CARDANO
ADA
NETWORK
AND
WEB-3.0

GTSTARR

Table of Contents

Introduction to Blockchain and Cryptocurrencies

Blockchain and cryptocurrencies have become buzzwords in recent years, with more and more people curious about their potential impact on various industries. Simply put, blockchain is a decentralized digital ledger that records transactions in a secure and transparent manner. It uses a network of computers to verify and add to the ledger, making it difficult to alter or manipulate data.

Cryptocurrencies, on the other hand, are digital or virtual currencies that use cryptography to secure and verify transactions, as well as to control the creation of new units. Bitcoin, the first and most well-known cryptocurrency, was created in 2009 by an unknown person or group using the pseudonym Satoshi Nakamoto. Since then, numerous other cryptocurrencies have been created, each with its own unique features and use cases.

One of the most appealing aspects of blockchain and cryptocurrencies is their potential to disrupt traditional financial systems and provide greater financial inclusion to individuals and businesses. However, there are also concerns around their security, regulation, and volatility.

Blockchain technology is essentially a distributed database that stores a growing list of records called blocks, which are linked together and secured using cryptography. Each block contains a cryptographic hash of the previous block, a timestamp, and transaction data. This makes it very difficult for anyone to tamper with the data, since any changes to one block would require changes to all subsequent blocks in the chain.

Cryptocurrencies, as mentioned earlier, are digital or virtual currencies that use blockchain technology to secure and verify transactions. They are decentralized, meaning they are not controlled by any central authority, such as a government or financial institution. This has led to their popularity as a way to make transactions without the need for a middleman.

There are several types of cryptocurrencies, including Bitcoin, Ethereum, Ripple, and Litecoin, each with its own unique features and uses. Some cryptocurrencies are designed for faster transactions, while others focus on privacy or energy efficiency. The market for cryptocurrencies is highly volatile, with prices fluctuating widely based on supply and demand.

One of the potential benefits of cryptocurrencies is their ability to provide greater financial inclusion to individuals and businesses that may not have access to traditional banking services. They can also provide a way to securely and quickly transfer funds across borders without the need for intermediaries or high fees.

However, there are also concerns around the security and regulation of cryptocurrencies. Since they are decentralized, they are vulnerable to hacking and other security breaches. Governments and financial institutions are also grappling with how to regulate this new form of currency, with some countries banning or heavily regulating cryptocurrencies, while others are embracing them as a way to spur innovation and economic growth.

Overall, blockchain and cryptocurrencies are fascinating technologies with the potential to disrupt various industries and change the way we think about money and transactions. As they continue to evolve and mature, it will be interesting to see how they are adopted and used in the years to come. Blockchain and cryptocurrencies are exciting new technologies that have also the potential to revolutionize web 3.0 technology, and their impact is still being explored and developed. One of those revolutionary blockchain being discussed in this guide is Cardano-ADA, third generation blockchain and a Web 3.0 technology!

Chapter 1
Web 3.0 Technology

Web3 refers to the next generation of the internet, where users have more control over their data and online identity. It is built on decentralized technology such as blockchain, and aims to create a more open and transparent internet.

Web3, also known as Web 3.0, is the next generation of the internet where the emphasis is on decentralization, autonomy, and agency. Unlike the current web, which is primarily controlled by a small number of large companies and organizations, web3 is built on decentralized technologies such as blockchain and peer-to-peer networks, which enable individuals and communities to have more control over their online interactions and data. This allows for the creation of decentralized applications (dApps) and new business models that were not possible before. Web3 is still in its early stages of development and is expected to bring significant changes to the way we interact and transact online.

Web3 is the evolution of the current internet, which is primarily centralized and controlled by a small number of large companies and organizations. Web3, on the other hand, is built on decentralized technologies such as blockchain and peer-to-peer networks. This allows for the creation of decentralized applications (dApps) which are open-source, trustless and transparent, and enables users to interact with the apps without the need for a trusted intermediary.

One of the main features of web3 is the use of blockchain technology to create decentralized systems. Blockchain is a distributed ledger technology that allows multiple parties to maintain and update a shared database without the need for a central authority. This enables the creation of decentralized systems such as decentralized finance (DeFi) platforms, decentralized marketplaces, and decentralized social networks, among others.

Another key feature of web3 is the use of smart contracts, which are self-executing contracts with the terms of the agreement between buyer and seller being directly written into lines of code. Smart contracts enable the creation of trustless and transparent transactions, as well as the creation of new business models such as tokenized assets and decentralized autonomous organizations (DAOs).

Web3 also aims to give users more control over their personal data and online interactions. With web3, users can own and control their data, rather than having to rely on centralized platforms to store and manage it for them. This can enable new business models such as decentralized data marketplaces where users can monetize their data. Web3 is still in its early stages of development and is expected to bring significant changes to the way we interact and transact online. However, it is important to note that web3 is not a finished product and many of the technologies and ideas behind it are still being developed and tested.

On September 13, 2021, the successful deployment of the Alonzo hard fork marked a significant milestone for Cardano. This upgrade introduced Plutus-powered smart contract functionality, making it possible for the network to support DeFi, DApp, and general web3 functional ecosystems, which are crucial for any blockchain platform.

Before the Alonzo upgrade, Cardano had been criticized for being "the smart contract platform with no smart contracts," with some even referring to it as a "ghost chain." However, with the deployment of Alonzo, Cardano now allows anyone with the ability to create and deploy their smart contracts and DApps on the blockchain, resulting in a surge in developer activity.

Chapter 2
What is Cardano ADA?

Cardano is a decentralized, open-source blockchain platform that is powered by the native cryptocurrency, ADA. It was created in 2015 by blockchain development firm Input Output Hong Kong (IOHK) and is led by Charles Hoskinson, co-founder of Ethereum. Cardano is built on a proof-of-stake (PoS) consensus algorithm and uses a unique multi-layered architecture that separates the settlement layer and the control layer, allowing for the creation of smart contracts and decentralized applications (DApps). Cardano is designed to be a more secure and scalable platform for the creation and execution of smart contracts and DApps, with a focus on privacy and regulatory compliance. It is also designed to be more energy-efficient than proof-of-work (PoW) blockchain platforms, such as Bitcoin and Ethereum.

Cardano works by using a proof-of-stake (PoS) consensus algorithm to validate transactions and add them to the blockchain. In a PoS system, validators ("stakeholders") are chosen to create new blocks based on the amount of ADA they hold in stake. This is in contrast to proof-of-work (PoW) systems, where miners are chosen to create new blocks based on their ability to solve complex mathematical problems (and are rewarded with a certain amount of cryptocurrency for their efforts).

In the Cardano platform, the creation of new blocks is managed by a system called "Ouroboros," which determines how individual stakeholders will be chosen to validate transactions and add them to the blockchain. The Ouroboros system is designed to be highly secure and efficient, and it ensures that the distribution of stakes among stakeholders is fair.

One of the key features of Cardano is its use of a multi-layered architecture, which separates the settlement layer and the control layer. The settlement layer is responsible for the transfer of value, while the control layer is responsible for the execution of smart contracts and the creation of decentralized applications (DApps). This separation of responsibilities allows for greater flexibility and scalability in the platform, as well as improved security.

Cardano also has a strong focus on privacy and regulatory compliance, and it uses a number of advanced cryptographic techniques to ensure the privacy and security of transactions on the platform. Overall, the goal of Cardano is to create a decentralized platform that is secure, scalable, and capable of handling a wide range of transactions and applications.

1. **Multi-layered architecture:** Cardano has a unique multi-layered architecture that separates the settlement layer and the control layer, allowing for greater flexibility and scalability in the platform.

2. **Proof-of-stake consensus algorithm:** Cardano uses a proof-of-stake (PoS) consensus algorithm, which means that validators ("stakeholders") are chosen to create new blocks based on the amount of ADA they hold in stake. This is in contrast to proof-of-work (PoW) systems, which use miners to create new blocks.

3. **Focus on security and regulatory compliance:** Cardano has a strong focus on security and regulatory compliance, and it uses advanced cryptographic techniques to ensure the privacy and security of transactions on the platform.

4. **Energy efficiency**: Cardano is designed to be more energy-efficient than other proof-of-work blockchain platforms, such as Bitcoin and Ethereum.

5. **Development team:** Cardano is developed by Input Output Hong Kong (IOHK), a highly respected blockchain development firm, and is led by Charles Hoskinson, co-founder of Ethereum.

Cardano is a decentralized platform that enables a variety of functions, including smart contracts, non-fungible token (NFT) minting, secure and fast data communication with proof of authenticity, interoperability between blockchains, staking and delegation, decentralized exchanges and automated market makers (AMMs), application development, a growing ecosystem, and a community of participants. Cardano can be used to facilitate the transfer of medical records, proof of ownership for assets such as houses, the sale of unique digital assets like art and books, and the exchange of cryptocurrencies across different blockchains. It also has the potential to serve as a stablecoin, support banking and business platforms, enable transparent and accurate voting, and store valuable data that is resistant to decay or manipulation. Overall, Cardano is a disruptive and innovative technology that offers a wide range of applications and opportunities for participation.

Cardano is designed to be an upgradeable platform, with a focus on interoperability and extensibility. This means that the Cardano platform can be easily modified and improved over time, and it can also be integrated with other blockchain platforms.

Cardano is a blockchain platform that aims to provide a more secure, scalable and sustainable infrastructure for the development of decentralized applications (dApps) and smart contracts. As a web3 platform, Cardano has several features that set it apart from other blockchain platforms:

Scientific approach: Cardano is built on a foundation of research and scientific rigor, with a focus on addressing key issues such as scalability, interoperability, and governance.

Proof-of-stake consensus: Cardano uses a proof-of-stake (PoS) consensus mechanism, which is more energy-efficient than proof-of-work (PoW) mechanisms used by other platforms such as Bitcoin.

Multi-layer architecture: Cardano has a multi-layer architecture that separates the computation layer from the settlement layer, allowing for more flexibility and scalability in the design of dApps and smart contracts.

Pluggable governance: Cardano has a governance system that allows for the community to make decisions on the future development of the platform, as well as the ability to upgrade the protocol in a decentralized way.

Interoperability: Cardano aims to enable interoperability between different blockchain platforms, which would allow for the easy exchange of value and data across different networks.

Formal verification: Cardano's smart contract language, Plutus, allows for the use of formal verification, a method of mathematically proving the correctness of code. This can increase the security and reliability of smart contracts on the platfo

Cardano has a strong focus on research and development, and it has a dedicated team of researchers and developers who are constantly working on improving and expanding the platform.

Cardano is an actively developed platform, with regular updates and improvements being released. The Cardano community also plays a large role in the development and direction of the platform, with community input being taken into account when making decisions about the future of the platform.

Cardano has a number of partnerships and collaborations with leading organizations in various industries, including government, education, and finance. These partnerships help to promote the adoption and use of Cardano in a variety of sectors.

Cardano has a large and active community of users and developers, with a wide range of resources and support available for those interested in learning more about the platform.

ADA is the native cryptocurrency of the Cardano blockchain platform. It is used to facilitate transactions on the Cardano platform and can also be used as a store of value. Some other key points about ADA include:

The name "Ada" is not an acronym; it was chosen in honor of Augusta Ada Lovelace (1815-1852), a mathematician who is sometimes regarded as the world's first programmer because of her work with Charles Babbage. ADA was created in 2015, along with the Cardano platform. ADA is traded on a number of cryptocurrency exchanges and can be purchased with a variety of fiat currencies and other cryptocurrencies.The total supply of ADA is fixed at 45 billion coins, with approximately 35.05 billion in circulation as of March 2023. The price of ADA is determined by market supply and demand, and it can fluctuate significantly over time.ADA is used to facilitate transactions on the Cardano platform, and it can also be used to participate in the proof-of-stake (PoS) consensus process that underlies the Cardano blockchain.ADA holders can earn a return on their investment by participating in the PoS process and helping to validate transactions on the Cardano network.ADA is designed to be a stable and secure cryptocurrency, with a focus on compliance and regulatory requirements.

Cardano can be used in a number of ways, including:

1. **Transactions**: Cardano can be used to facilitate fast and secure transactions between users.

2. **Smart contracts**: Cardano's control layer allows for the creation and execution of smart contracts, which are self-executing contracts with the terms of the agreement between buyer and seller being directly written into lines of code.

3. **Decentralized applications**:(DApps): Cardano's control layer also allows for the creation of decentralized applications (DApps), which are applications that run on a decentralized network and are not controlled by any single entity.

4. **Staking**: ADA holders can earn a return on their investment by participating in the proof-of-stake (PoS) consensus process that underlies the Cardano blockchain.

5. **Store of value**: Like other cryptocurrencies, ADA can be used as a store of value and as a means of exchange.

Overall, Cardano is a versatile platform that can be used for a wide range of purposes, including transactions, smart contracts, decentralized applications, and more.

Cardano is an open-source platform, which means that its source code is available for anyone to view and modify. This helps to ensure transparency and security on the platform.

Cardano is a global platform, with users and developers located all around the world. It is designed to be accessible and usable by people of all backgrounds and technical skill levels.

Cardano has a strong focus on education and outreach, with a number of resources available for those who want to learn more about the platform and how to use it. This includes a comprehensive documentation library, as well as a number of community-led initiatives and educational materials.

Cardano has a number of partnerships and collaborations with leading organizations in various industries, including government, education, and finance. These partnerships help to promote the adoption and use of Cardano in a variety of sectors.

Cardano has a large and active community of users and developers, with a wide range of resources and support available for those interested in learning more about the platform.

Cardano is an open-source platform, which means that its source code is available for anyone to view and modify. This helps to ensure transparency and security on the platform.

Cardano is a global platform, with users and developers located all around the world. It is designed to be accessible and usable by people of all backgrounds and technical skill levels.

Cardano has a strong focus on education and outreach, with a number of resources available for those who want to learn more about the platform and how to use it. This includes a comprehensive documentation library, as well as a number of community-led initiatives and educational materials.

Cardano has a number of partnerships and collaborations with leading organizations in various industries, including government, education, and finance. These partnerships help to promote the adoption and use of Cardano in a variety of sectors.

Cardano has a large and active community of users and developers, with a wide range of resources and support available for those interested in learning more about the platform.

Cardano is built on a proof-of-stake (PoS) consensus algorithm, which means that validators ("stakeholders") are chosen to create new blocks based on the amount of ADA they hold in stake. This is in contrast to proof-of-work (PoW) systems, which use miners to create new blocks.

Cardano uses a system called "Ouroboros" to manage the creation of new blocks and ensure the distribution of stakes among stakeholders is fair. Ouroboros is a highly secure and efficient system that is designed to be resistant to attacks and ensure the integrity of the Cardano blockchain.

Ouroboros is the name of the proof-of-stake (PoS) consensus algorithm used by the Cardano blockchain platform. It is the first PoS algorithm that has been proven to be fully secure in the random oracle model, which is a standard model used to analyze cryptographic protocols.

In a PoS system, validators ("stakeholders") are chosen to create new blocks based on the amount of ADA they hold in stake. These validators are responsible for verifying the transactions included in a new block and ensuring that they are valid and conform to the rules of the Cardano platform.

Ouroboros has a number of features that make it well-suited for use on the Cardano platform:

Security: Ouroboros is the first PoS algorithm that has been proven to be fully secure in the random oracle model, which makes it highly resistant to attacks.

Efficiency: Ouroboros is designed to be highly efficient, with a low overhead and minimal resource requirements. This makes it well-suited for use on resource-constrained devices such as mobile phones.

Scalability: Ouroboros is designed to be highly scalable, with the ability to handle a large number of transactions and applications simultaneously. This makes it well-suited for use on a global, decentralized platform like Cardano. Overall, Ouroboros is an important part of the Cardano platform and plays a key role in ensuring the security, efficiency, and scalability of the network.

Cardano has a number of advanced features designed to improve security and scalability on the platform, including cryptographic techniques such as secure multiparty computation (SMC) and delegated proof-of-stake (DPoS), which help to protect the privacy of users and prevent unauthorized access to sensitive data.

In addition, Cardano has a number of features that are designed to improve the security of smart contracts, which are self-executing contracts with the terms of the agreement between buyer and seller being directly written into lines of code. These features include formal verification, which allows developers to mathematically prove the correctness of their code, and a modular design, which allows different components of the platform to be easily replaced or upgraded. Overall, Cardano is designed to be a secure and reliable platform for the development and execution of smart contracts, and it includes a number of features and tools to ensure the privacy and security of transactions on the platform.

Cardano is constantly being improved and updated, with regular updates and improvements being released to the platform. The Cardano community also plays a large role in the development and direction of the platform, with community input being taken into account when making decisions about the future of the platform.

Cardano has a strong focus on research and development, and it has a dedicated team of researchers and developers who are constantly working on improving and expanding the platform. This includes partnerships with leading research institutions and universities around the world.

Cardano is the first blockchain platform to be built using the Haskell programming language. Haskell is a functional programming language that is widely used in academia and is known for its strong emphasis on security and reliability.

Cardano is designed to be highly modular and customizable, with a modular design that allows different components of the platform to be easily replaced or upgraded. This helps to ensure the long-term sustainability and flexibility of the platform.

Cardano has a number of advanced features that are not yet fully implemented, but are planned for future development. These include features such as atomic swaps, which will allow users to exchange different cryptocurrencies directly without the need for intermediaries, and smart wallets, which will enable users to manage their digital assets more securely and easily.

In summary, Cardano is a web3 platform that aims to provide a more secure, scalable, sustainable and governance-friendly infrastructure for the development of decentralized applications and smart contracts. It also aims to provide a solution for interoperability, which could be a key feature in the future of decentralized networks.

Chapter 3
Cardano Development

Cardano is being developed in a series of phases, each of which focuses on a specific set of features and improvements. The phases of Cardano development are:

Byron: The first phase of Cardano development, which focused on the creation of the Cardano platform and the launch of the mainnet. The Byron phase of Cardano development was the first phase of the project, and it focused on the creation of the Cardano platform and the launch of the mainnet. Some key points about the Byron phase include: The Byron phase began in 2015 and was completed in 2017.During the Byron phase, the Cardano platform was developed and the mainnet was launched.The main goal of the Byron phase was to create a stable and secure platform that could be used for a wide range of transactions and applications.The Byron phase also included the creation of the native cryptocurrency, ADA, and the implementation of the proof-of-stake (PoS) consensus algorithm.The Byron phase laid the foundation for the development of the

Cardano platform and set the stage for the subsequent phases of development.

Shelley: The second phase of Cardano development, which focuses on decentralized governance and the decentralization of the platform. This phase also includes the introduction of staking and the ability for users to delegate their stake to validators.The Shelley phase of Cardano development is the second phase of the project, and it focuses on decentralized governance and the decentralization of the platform. Some key points about the Shelley phase include: The Shelley phase began in 2019 and is ongoing.During the Shelley phase, the Cardano platform is being transitioned from a centralized system to a decentralized one. This includes the introduction of staking, which allows users to delegate their stake to validators and earn a return on their investment. The main goal of the Shelley phase is to increase the decentralization of the Cardano platform and give more power and control to the community.The Shelley phase also includes the implementation of new features and improvements to the platform, such as the ability to update the protocol without the need for a hard fork.The Shelley phase is an important step in the development of Cardano and will help to ensure the long-term stability and security of the platform.

Goguen: The third phase of Cardano development, which focuses on the integration of smart contracts and the creation of decentralized applications (DApps). The Goguen phase of Cardano development is the third phase of the project, and it focuses on the integration of smart contracts and the creation of decentralized applications (DApps). Some key points about the Goguen phase include: The Goguen phase is expected to begin in 2021.During the Goguen phase, the Cardano platform will be updated to support the creation and execution of smart contracts. This will allow developers to build and deploy a wide range of decentralized applications (DApps) on the platform.The main goal of the Goguen phase is to expand the capabilities of the Cardano platform and make it more versatile and useful for a wide range of applications.The Goguen phase will also include the implementation of new features and improvements to the platform, such as the ability to support multiple virtual machines and languages.The Goguen phase is an important step in the development of Cardano and will help to increase the adoption and use of the platform.

Basho: The fourth phase of Cardano development, which focuses on improving the performance and scalability of the platform. The Basho phase is expected to begin in 2021.During the Basho phase, the Cardano platform will be optimized and updated to improve performance and scalability. This will include the implementation of new technologies and The Basho phase is expected to begin in 2021.During the Basho phase, the Cardano platform will be optimized and updated to improve performance and scalability. This will include the implementation of new technologies and techniques to increase the speed and efficiency of the platform.The main goal of the Basho phase is to make the Cardano platform more usable and accessible to a wider audience. The Basho phase will also include the implementation of new features and improvements to the platform, such as support for off-chain transactions and other advanced features. The Basho phase is an important step in the development of Cardano and will help to increase the adoption and use of the platform.

Voltaire: The fifth and final phase of Cardano development, which focuses on decentralized governance and the ability for the community to fund and govern the development of the platform.The

Voltaire phase of Cardano development is the fifth and final phase of the project, and it focuses on decentralized governance and the ability for the community to fund and govern the development of the platform. Some key points about the Voltaire phase include: The Voltaire phase is expected to begin in 2022.During the Voltaire phase, the Cardano platform will be updated to support decentralized governance and the ability for the community to fund and govern the development of the platform. This will include the implementation of a voting and proposal system that allows the community to have a say in the direction of the platform. The main goal of the Voltaire phase is to give the Cardano community more control and ownership over the platform and ensure that it is transparent and accountable. The Voltaire phase will also include the implementation of new features and improvements to the platform, such as support for new programming languages and improved interoperability with other blockchain platforms.The Voltaire phase is the final step in the development of Cardano and will help to ensure the long-term stability and success of the platform.

Cardano is an actively developed platform, with regular updates and improvements being released as each phase is completed. The development of Cardano is overseen by Input Output Hong Kong (IOHK), a blockchain development firm, and is led by Charles Hoskinson, co-founder of Ethereum.

Chapter 4
Cardano VS Bitcoin decentralization

In the Bitcoin network, transactions are validated through a process called "mining," in which miners use specialized computers to solve complex mathematical problems and add new blocks to the blockchain. Because mining requires a lot of resources and energy, it is typically done by a small number of large entities on a global scale, which makes the Bitcoin network somewhat centralized.

Cardano, on the other hand, uses a proof-of-stake (PoS) consensus algorithm to validate transactions and add them to the blockchain. In a PoS system, validators ("stakeholders") are chosen to create new blocks based on the amount of ADA they hold in stake. This process does not require mining and is much less resource-intensive than the PoW algorithm used by Bitcoin.

Cardano has a large number of stake pools and validator nodes, which makes it one of the most decentralized cryptocurrencies. The Cardano foundation and its founders hold a relatively small percentage of the total supply of ADA, with most of the coins being held by the community. Users can delegate their ADA to stake pools and receive rewards for helping to secure and run the network. Cardano also has mechanisms in place to prevent centralization and allow the network to recover if too much control is concentrated in a few hands. Despite this, Cardano can still be affected by market volatility like other cryptocurrencies.

It is not accurate to say that one cryptocurrency is "more decentralized" or "less decentralized" than another in an absolute sense. Decentralization is a relative concept and can vary depending on the specific characteristics and design of a given cryptocurrency

In the case of Bitcoin and Cardano, both cryptocurrencies use different consensus algorithms and have different structures and properties that affect their degree of decentralization. For example, Bitcoin uses a proof-of-work (PoW) consensus algorithm, which requires miners to use specialized computers to solve complex mathematical problems in order to validate transactions and add new blocks to the blockchain. This process is resource-intensive and is typically done by a small number of large entities on a global scale, which makes the Bitcoin network somewhat centralized.

Cardano, on the other hand, uses a proof-of-stake (PoS) consensus algorithm, in which validators ("stakeholders") are chosen to create new blocks based on the amount of ADA they hold in stake. This process does not require mining and is much less resource-intensive than the PoW algorithm used by Bitcoin. Cardano also has a large number of stake pools and validator nodes, which makes it one of the most decentralized cryptocurrencies.

Overall, it is not accurate to say that Cardano is "less decentralized" than Bitcoin. Both cryptocurrencies have different characteristics and design choices that affect their degree of decentralization, and it is important to consider these differences when evaluating their relative decentralization

Chapter 5
Eco Friendly and Energy Efficient

Proof-Of-Stake And Proof-Of-Work

There are two main blockchain protocols: proof-of-stake (PoS) and proof-of-work (PoW). These protocols are consensus algorithms for distributed networks: rulesets that dictate how networks – made up of thousands of nodes – agree on new additions (blocks) in a permissionless setting.

Proof-of-work is the blockchain protocol used by bitcoin. Proof-of-work began a revolution: it enabled the creation of secure, permissionless, distributed networks. But to achieve consensus for each new block, proof-of-work requires an enormous amount of energy: an amount so large that the supported blockchains struggle to sustain and scale to the performance requirements of global networks.

Proof-of-stake answers the performance and energy-use challenges of proof-of-work, and arrives at a more sustainable solution. Instead of relying on 'miners' to solve computationally complex equations to create new blocks – and rewarding the first to do so – proof of stake selects participants (in the case of Cardano, stake pools) to create new blocks based on the stake they control in the network.

This enables networks to scale horizontally, increasing performance by incorporating additional nodes, rather than vertically, through the addition of more powerful hardware. The resulting difference in energy use can be analogized to that between a household and a small country. PoS is positioned scale to the mass market; PoW is not.

Cardano is designed to be energy-efficient and have a low environmental impact. One of the ways that it achieves this is through its proof-of-stake (PoS) consensus algorithm, which is used to validate transactions and add them to the blockchain.

In a proof-of-work (PoW) system, such as Bitcoin, miners use computing power to solve complex mathematical problems in order to create new blocks and validate transactions. This process, known as mining, requires a large amount of energy, as miners must constantly run their computers to compete for the right to create a new block.

In contrast, a PoS does not require miners to solve complex mathematical problems in order to create new blocks. Instead, validators ("stakeholders") are chosen to create new blocks based on the amount of ADA they hold in stake. This process uses significantly less energy than PoW systems, as it does not require miners to constantly run their computers to compete for block rewards.

Energy Efficient

Ouroboros solves the greatest challenge faced by existing blockchains: the need for more and more energy to achieve consensus. Using Ouroboros, Cardano is able to securely, sustainably, and ethically scale, with up to four million times the energy efficiency of bitcoin. Ouroboros ensures the continuity of each moment: the incremental building of an unbreakable chain. Through it, every addition – transaction, agreement, sharing of information – becomes part of an immutable past.

Cardano has a strong focus on sustainability and environmental responsibility, and it includes features such as carbon offsetting to reduce the environmental impact of the platform

Chapter 6
Staking Pools and Rewards

Incentives & Rewards

To ensure the sustainability of the blockchain networks using Ouroboros, the Cardano protocol features an incentive mechanism that rewards network participants for their participation.This can either be operating a stake pool or delegating a stake in ada to a stake pool. Rewards (in the form of ada) can be earned by completing either of these activities.

Stake Delegation And Stake Pools

Cardano's Ouroboros is a proof-of-stake protocol. It distributes network control across stake pools: node operators with the infrastructure required to ensure a consistent and reliable connection to the network.

For each slot, a stake pool is assigned as the slot leader, and is rewarded for adding a block to the chain. Ada holders may delegate their stake to a specific stake pool, increasing its chance of being selected as the slot leader, and share in the stake pool's rewards.

How Ouroboros Works

Ouroboros processes transaction blocks by dividing chains into epochs, which are further divided into time slots. A slot leader is elected for each time slot and is responsible for adding a block to the chain. To protect against adversarial attempts to subvert the protocol, each new slot leader is required to consider the last few blocks of the received chain as transient: only the chain that precedes a prespecified number of transient blocks is considered settled. This is also referred to as the settlement delay, and is the mechanism through which the ledger is securely passed between participants.

Ouroboros is a meld of innovative technology and philosophy. Its research explores how we behave as a society, to discover an ideal balance - defined through game theory - between individual and collective interests. Ouroboros' incentive mechanism rewards participants for their honest participation, and disincentivizes dishonest actors. It is a stable and sustainable foundation for permission networks that are built to endure: the infrastructure of the future.

Validators

In the Cardano blockchain, network validation is the process by which transactions are verified and added to the blockchain. This process is essential to the security and integrity of the network and helps to ensure that only valid transactions are included in the blockchain.

On the Cardano network, network validation is performed by a group of special nodes called "validators." Validators are responsible for verifying the transactions included in a new block and ensuring that they are valid and conform to the rules of the Cardano platform.

To become a validator on the Cardano network, a node must "stake" a certain amount of ADA, which is the native cryptocurrency of the Cardano platform. The more ADA a node has staked, the more likely it is to be chosen as a validator.

Validators are chosen to create new blocks based on their stake and a random selection process. Once a validator has been chosen to create a new block, they are responsible for collecting and verifying the transactions that are included in the block. If a validator tries to include invalid or malicious transactions in a block, they may lose their stake as punishment, which provides an incentive for them to act in the best interests of the network.

Overall, network validation is an important part of the Cardano platform and helps to ensure the security and integrity of the network by verifying the validity of transactions before they are added to the blockchain.

Delegator

Delegating Cardano refers to the process of allowing another individual or entity to act as a representative and perform certain tasks on your behalf on the Cardano platform.On the Cardano platform, delegating is mainly used in the context of the proof-of-stake (PoS) consensus algorithm, which is used to validate transactions and add them to the blockchain. In a PoS system, validators ("stakeholders") are chosen to create new blocks based on the amount of ADA they hold in stake. These validators are responsible for verifying the transactions included in a new block and ensuring that they are valid and conform to the rules of the Cardano platform.

To become a validator on the Cardano network, a node must "stake" a certain amount of ADA. However, not everyone who holds ADA may want or be able to participate in the validation process as a validator. In these cases, users can choose to delegate their stake to another individual or entity who will act as their representative and participate in the validation process on their behalf.

Delegating is a simple process that can be done through a variety of tools and platforms. Once a user has delegated their stake, they can still retain control over their ADA and can choose to undelegate or change their delegate at any time.

Overall, delegating is a useful feature that allows users to participate in the validation process on the Cardano network without having to stake their own ADA or become a validator themselves.

Stake pools

On the Cardano platform, a stake pool is a group of users who combine their resources in order to earn rewards. Stake pools can be either public or private. Public stake pools can be delegated to by anyone and offer rewards to delegators, while private stake pools only distribute rewards to their owners. Users who do not want to operate a node themselves can delegate their stake to a public stake pool and receive rewards based on the pool's performance.

To operate a stake pool, an individual or business must have the knowledge and resources to run a Cardano network node consistently. Ada holders who do not wish to run a node themselves can delegate their stake to a public stake pool and receive rewards based on the pool's performance. The more stake that is delegated to a stake pool, the greater the chance it has of being chosen as a validator and producing blocks on the blockchain.

The rewards earned by a stake pool are shared between the stake pool operator and the delegators. Technical parameters, such as the amount of stake and the resources invested, influence the rewards received by stake pools and help to ensure a fair and competitive marketplace. Extensive research and development have gone into the design of the stake pool system in order to incentivize participation and fairly reward the investment of time, energy, and resources.

Pledging Mechanism

On the Cardano platform, pool operators can choose to pledge some or all of their stake to their pool in order to make it more attractive to potential delegators. The amount of ada pledged to a pool has an influence on the rewards that the pool will receive, and pools with higher amounts of ada pledged tend to be more protocol parameter "a0" determines the impact of the pledge on the pool's reward. While there is no minimum pledge amount required, pool operators can choose to pledge an amount that they believe will be most effective at attracting delegation to their pool.

Desirability Index

The attractiveness of a stake pool on the Cardano platform is determined by a combination of factors, including the amount of ada pledged by the pool operator, the costs associated with running the pool, the margin earned by the pool, and the pool's performance and saturation level. This information is used to rank pools in terms of their desirability to potential delegators and is displayed in Daedalus and Yoroi, Cardano's official wallet applications. By considering these factors, delegators can choose the stake pools that they believe will offer the best rewards and support the overall security and performance of the Cardano network.

Saturation Parameter (K)

Saturation is a concept in the Cardano platform that refers to the point at which a stake pool has more stake delegated to it than is optimal for the network. Saturation is measured in terms of the "k" parameter, which represents the target number of desired pools. When a stake pool reaches the point of saturation, it will offer diminishing rewards to delegators. The saturation mechanism is designed to prevent centralization by encouraging delegators to spread their stake across multiple pools and to incentivize pool operators to set up new pools in order to continue earning maximum rewards. This helps to preserve the interests of both ada holders who delegate their stake and pool operators, and prevents any single pool from becoming too large and dominant. Overall, the saturation mechanism is intended to promote a healthy, decentralized network by balancing the interests of all stakeholders.

Decentralization Parameter

The decentralization parameter is a tunable setting that is used to control the ratio of slots (positions in the blockchain that can be filled by new blocks) created by federation nodes (a group of trusted nodes that are responsible for coordinating the transition to the Shelley era) versus those created by stake pool nodes (groups of users who pool their resources in order to increase their chances of being chosen as validators). This parameter will be used during the early stages of the deployment of Shelley, the next major update to the Cardano platform, on the mainnet (the live Cardano network). It is important to note that during this transition period, all rewards will be distributed to operating stake pools and not to the federation nodes. The decentralization parameter is being implemented in order to allow the network to stabilize and ensure a smooth transition to the Shelley era. This parameter helps to balance the interests of all stakeholders and promote a decentralized network structure.

Chapter 7
Security

Cardano is designed to be secure and resistant to attacks on the network. It uses a number of techniques and technologies to ensure the security and integrity of the platform. One key aspect of the security of Cardano is its proof-of-stake (PoS) consensus algorithm, which is used to validate transactions and add them to the blockchain. In a PoS system, validators ("stakeholders") are chosen to create new blocks based on the amount of ADA they hold in stake. These validators are responsible for verifying the transactions included in a new block and ensuring that they are valid and conform to the rules of the Cardano platform.

The PoS consensus algorithm helps to ensure the security of the Cardano network in a number of ways:

Decentralization: Cardano is a decentralized platform, with a large number of validators participating in the network. This helps to ensure that no single entity has control over the network and makes it more resistant to attacks.

Staking: Validators on the Cardano network must "stake" a certain amount of ADA in order to in the validation process. If a validator acts maliciously or tries to attack the network, they stand to lose their stake, which provides an incentive for them to act in the best interests of the network.

Slashing: Cardano has a "slashing" mechanism in place that punishes validators who act maliciously or try to attack the network. If a validator is found to be acting in a way that is detrimental to the network, they may lose part or all of their stake, which helps to discourage malicious behavior.

In addition to its PoS consensus algorithm, Cardano also uses a number of other techniques and technologies to improve security on the network:

Cryptographic techniques: Cardano uses advanced cryptographic techniques, such as secure multiparty computation (SMC) and delegated proof-of-stake (DPoS), to ensure the privacy and security of transactions on the platform.

Layered architecture: Cardano is built on a layered architecture, with a separate layer for the settlement layer (which handles transactions) and a control layer (which handles smart contracts and DApps). This separation of concerns helps to improve the security and scalability of the platform.

Code review: Cardano has a thorough code review process in place to ensure the quality and security of the platform's codebase. This includes both internal and external review, with code being reviewed by a team of experienced developers before being deployed to the network.

Bug bounty programs: Cardano has a number of bug bounty programs in place to encourage members of the community to report vulnerabilities or issues with the platform. These programs provide rewards to users who report bugs or vulnerabilities, which helps to improve the overall security of the platform.

Overall, Cardano is designed to be a secure and reliable platform, and it uses a number of techniques and technologies to ensure the security and integrity of the network.

The PoS consensus algorithm helps to prevent 51% attacks in a number of ways:

Decentralization: Cardano is a decentralized platform, with a large number of validators participating in the network. This makes it more difficult for a single entity or group of entities to control more than 51% of the network's computing power. Cardano is designed to be resistant to 51% attacks, which are a type of attack on a blockchain network in which a single entity or group of entities controls more than half of the network's computing power. If an attacker is able to control more than 51% of the network's computing power, they can potentially disrupt the network, censor transactions, or double spend coins. One of the main ways that Cardano prevents 51% attacks is through its proof-of-stake (PoS) consensus algorithm. In a PoS system, validators ("stakeholders") are chosen to create new blocks based on the amount of ADA they hold in stake. These validators are responsible for verifying the transactions included in a new block and ensuring that they are valid and conform to the rules of the Cardano platform.

Overall, the combination of decentralization, staking, and slashing helps to make Cardano resistant to 51% attacks and ensure the security and integrity.

Chapter 8
CVM and Plutus

The Cardano Virtual Machine (CVM) is a decentralized virtual machine that is designed to execute smart contracts and decentralized applications (DApps) on the Cardano platform. The CVM is implemented on the control layer of the Cardano blockchain and is responsible for executing the code of smart contracts and DApps in a secure and efficient manner. The CVM is designed to be highly secure and resistant to tampering or attacks, and it uses advanced cryptographic techniques to ensure the integrity and reliability of smart contracts and DApps. It is also designed to be highly scalable, with the ability to handle a large number of transactions and applications simultaneously. To use the CVM, a developer must first write the code for a smart contract or DApp using a programming language such as Plutus. The code is then compiled and deployed to the CVM, where it can be accessed and executed by users. The CVM is responsible for executing the code of the contract or DApp and ensuring that it is carried out according to the terms of the agreement. The CVM is an important component of the Cardano platform, and it enables the creation and execution of a wide range of smart contracts and DApps. This helps to increase the versatility and usefulness of the Cardano platform and allows it to be used for a variety of applications.

Smart contracts are self-executing contracts with the terms of the agreement between buyer and seller being directly written into lines of code. They are designed to facilitate, verify, and enforce the negotiation or performance of a contract.

On the Cardano platform, smart contracts are implemented on the control layer and are executed by the Cardano Virtual Machine (CVM). The CVM is a decentralized virtual machine that is designed to be secure and efficient, and it is capable of executing a wide range of smart contracts and decentralize applications (DApps). To create and deploy a smart contract on Cardano, a developer must first write the code for the contract using a programming language such as Plutus. The contract is then compiled and deployed to the Cardano blockchain, where it can be accessed and executed by users. Smart contracts on

Cardano have a number of features and benefits, including:

Automation: Smart contracts can be used to automate a wide range of processes, such as financial transactions, supply chain management, and more. This can help to reduce the need for manual intervention and streamline complex processes.

Transparency: Smart contracts are transparent and open to all users, which helps to ensure that the terms of the contract are clear and enforceable.

Security: Smart contracts are secured by the blockchain and are resistant to tampering or fraud. This helps to ensure the integrity and reliability of the contract.

Here are a few examples of how smart contracts could be used on the Cardano platform:

Financial transactions: A smart contract could be used to automate the transfer of funds between two parties based on the fulfillment of certain conditions. For example, a smart contract could be used to release payment for goods or services once they have been delivered.

Supply chain management: A smart contract could be used to automate the tracking and management of goods as they move through the supply chain. For example, a smart contract could be used to automatically release payment to a supplier once a shipment of goods has been received by the buyer.

Insurance: A smart contract could be used to automate the claims process for an insurance policy. For example, a smart contract could be used to automatically pay out a claim once the necessary documentation and conditions have been met.

Plutus is a programming language that is specifically designed for use on the Cardano platform. It is used to write smart contracts and decentralized applications (DApps) that can be executed on the Cardano Virtual Machine (CVM). Plutus is a functional programming language that is based on Haskell, a popular programming language for computer science research. It is designed to be expressive, modular, and secure, and it includes features such as type inference, higher-order functions, and parametric polymorphism. To use Plutus, a developer must first write the code for a smart contract or DApp using the Plutus language. The code is then compiled and deployed to the CVM, where it can be accessed and executed by users. Plutus is designed to be easy to use and learn, and it includes a range of tools and resources to help developers create and deploy smart contracts and DApps on the Cardano platform. Plutus is an important part of the Cardano platform, and it enables the creation and execution of a wide range of smart contracts and DApps. This helps to increase the versatility and usefulness of the Cardano platform and allows it to be used for a variety of applications.

There are a few reasons why Cardano chose to use Plutus as its programming language:

Security: Plutus is designed to be highly secure, with a focus on ensuring the integrity and reliability of smart contracts and DApps. It includes a range of features and tools to help developers create secure code, such as type inference and static analysis.

Compatibility: Plutus is specifically designed for use on the Cardano platform and is closely integrated with the Cardano Virtual Machine (CVM). This makes it easy for developers to create and deploy smart contracts and DApps on the Cardano platform.

Ease of use: Plutus is designed to be easy to use and learn, and it includes a range of tools and resources to help developers create and deploy smart contracts and DApps on the Cardano platform.

Overall, the use of Plutus as the programming language for Cardano helps to ensure the security and reliability of the platform, and it makes it easy for developers to create and deploy a wide range of smart contracts and DApps.

Chapter 9
Hydra

Hydra is a solution offered by Cardano to increase transaction speed, minimize transaction costs, and improve scalability. It operates as a layer 2 technology, utilizing low latency and high throughput to achieve its goals.

The first protocol in the Hydra family of protocols is known as Hydra Head. It serves as the foundation for more advanced deployment scenarios, particularly those that rely on isomorphic, multi-party state channels. Each Hydra Head operates as a mini ledger that is off-chain and shared among a small group of participants. By using Hydra Heads, developers can create specialized and complex protocols that sit on top of Cardano.

What's a low latency?

Low latency refers to the amount of time it takes for data to travel between its source and destination. In the context of computer networks and communication technologies, low latency means that there is minimal delay or lag time between when a user sends a request or command and when the system responds to it.

Low latency is important for many applications, especially those that require real-time data processing or immediate responses, such as online gaming, video conferencing, financial trading, and other time-sensitive activities. In the case of blockchain technology, low latency is crucial for improving transaction processing speed and reducing the time it takes for transactions to be confirmed and added to the blockchain.

What's a high throughput?

High throughput refers to the ability of a system or network to process a large volume of data or transactions in a given time period. In the context of blockchain technology, high throughput means that the blockchain network can handle a large number of transactions per second (TPS) without slowing down or causing delays.

High throughput is a crucial factor for blockchain scalability as it enables the network to support more users and applications while maintaining efficiency and reliability. A higher TPS means that more transactions can be processed in a shorter amount of time, which is essential for blockchain technology to be used for various applications beyond just digital currencies.

Several blockchain platforms, including Cardano, are exploring different approaches to improve throughput, such as sharding, off-chain scaling solutions, and layer 2 technologies like Hydra, to increase the number of transactions that can be processed simultaneously while maintaining network security and decentralization.

Hydra, also known as the Hydra Head Protocol, is a Cardano scalability solution that offers developers an open source framework to create off-chain ledgers. This framework can help developers use blockchain technology more efficiently.

The project is a collaborative effort between engineers at the Cardano Foundation and IOG. The code is publicly available, and the team welcomes contributions through a transparent process. Despite previous mentions of Hydra, there is still some confusion about its purpose and how it benefits the community. Therefore, it is important to review the basics of Hydra, its current status, and future plans.

Hydra is an isomorphic layer-2 solution that falls under the category of state-channel solutions. Essentially, a channel is a two-way communication link between multiple peers. In the context of blockchains, channels enable parties to exchange transactions without broadcasting them onto the main network. State-channels enable the creation of small networks that operate in parallel to the main network. This technology is a generalization of payment-channels, which were used to develop Bitcoin's Lightning Network layer-2 payment protocol, designed to facilitate faster transactions. However, state-channels support more complex transactions than payment-channels, including the execution of scripts, metadata, multi-assets UTxO, and more.

With Hydra, we can imagine a replicated section of the Cardano blockchain that operates independently from the main Cardano network and involves a limited number of participants. This allows users to conduct transactions at a faster pace on their private network, also known as their Hydra Head. Afterward, they can settle the results of their operations onto the main Cardano chain to inform the rest of the network about their interactions. This means that Hydra Heads can be established as needed in a semi-controlled environment by any actor requiring fast transaction speeds. We will provide additional examples later on.

In the world of distributed ledger technology (DLT), the base layer of a blockchain is referred to as layer-1, while layer-2 encompasses any solution or product developed on top of the mainchain. Layer-2 solutions often provide additional scalability to a blockchain. Therefore, since the Hydra Head protocol is constructed on top of the Cardano mainchain, it is considered a layer-2 solution

Moreover, Hydra is described as isomorphic because transactions in a Hydra Head possess the same capabilities as those on the Cardano network. The term "isomorphic" suggests this similarity since "iso-" means equal and "-morphic" refers to shape, form, or structure. In Mathematics, an isomorphism denotes a bi-directional mapping between elements from one domain to another while preserving their structural features. This means that transactions in a Hydra Head and on the Cardano network share a direct structural correspondence. Additionally, Hydra supports all programming languages supported by Cardano. Since Cardano allows the use of mainstream and specialized languages, transactions in Hydra can be developed using existing tooling familiar to developers.

In contrast to the Cardano mainchain, the Hydra Head ledger technology differs in consensus, transaction validation, and propagation among peers, with no stake pools involved. All participants of a head need to agree on every transaction, providing strong security guarantees but limiting the total number of participants in a single head. Despite common misconceptions, a hard fork does not enable Hydra, which remains a framework and infrastructure stack that projects running on Cardano can leverage to scale their use cases. Essentially, Hydra acts as a DApp for DApp developers seeking to scale their own protocols, comprising a set of on-chain scripts and a software stack named Hydra node that offers a high-level interface using widespread web technologies.

Over the past year, the Hydra team focused on ramping up software quality and preparing Hydra for the first pioneers to build. The team quantified limitations of the protocols through benchmarks, drafted CIP-0042, and extended its reach by embracing open source, maintaining a public roadmap, and launching a website. March witnessed the first Hydra Head open on a public testnet, and work commenced on the formalization of the Coordinated Head Protocol, along with integrating the new Babbage era introduced by the Vasil hard fork. The team also onboarded three new members, and builders announced exciting projects, including SundaeSwap Labs showcasing how they could run part of their protocol through a Hydra head, Obsidian Systems and IOG announcing Hydra for Payments, and TxPipe providing Hydra Head as a service through their platform Demeter. As interest in Hydra grows, the team is rethinking project goals and strategy for the future.

Future of Hydra

The Hydra project initially aimed to have 99% of all Cardano traffic happen off-chain in Hydra heads by November 2022. However, the team has set a new objective of becoming the number one DApp on Cardano by all known metrics, such as total value locked (TVL), traffic, volume, and other standards. The goal of increasing adoption and enabling growth in the Cardano ecosystem is shared by both objectives, but the second goal is more tangible and will drive the project's roadmap better.

Previously, Hydra was perceived as a solution to make Cardano faster, but the team wants to break away from this narrative and highlight that Hydra is, in essence, a DApp that requires integration and adoption to be truly useful.

In 2022, the main priority was gaining stability and facilitating easier onboarding for pioneers. In 2023, the focus will shift to adoption. The Hydra project always intended to support pioneers and help them get started, and many use cases have already been explored, such as payments, games, governance, and marketplaces. The end of 2022 showed how the first pioneers have begun to utilize the Hydra framework, and moving forward, the Hydra team intends to support them further and help new pioneers adopt Hydra as part of their toolstack.

Chapter 10
Cardano Partnerships

The Cardano Foundation is an autonomous organization that oversees and supervises the development of Cardano and its ecosystem. As the legal custodian of the protocol and owner of the Cardano brand, the Foundation strives to increase adoption and partnerships, foster the growth of the global Cardano community, shape legislation and commercial standards, and ensure accountability at all levels.

The Foundation's primary responsibility is to promote the adoption of the Cardano platform and support the diverse Cardano community, including individuals like you who engage with and implement ideas on the platform. To fulfill this role to the highest standards, the Cardano Foundation has a governing Council, a professional executive team, and community managers, many of whom are recruited directly from the wider Cardano community.

However, the Foundation's focus is not just inward-looking but also outward-looking. The

Foundation is equally committed to working with other key industries within the blockchain space, contributing to the advancement of the technology and driving adoption with other compatible systems. The Foundation participates in global discussions on blockchain technology, focusing on legal frameworks, integration with legacy systems and third-party applications, awareness, and education to ensure that blockchain technology is accessible and understandable to everyone.

EMURGO, one of the original members of the Cardano protocol, is a for-profit organization that focuses on developing, supporting, and incubating commercial opportunities to promote adoption of the Cardano blockchain system. With offices and active projects in Singapore, Japan, the USA, India, and Indonesia, EMURGO has extensive experience in blockchain R&D and a global network of partners in the blockchain industry.

EMURGO aims to support high-impact ideas that can positively transform various sectors such as finance, supply chain, retail, healthcare, public services, and IoT. As a comprehensive blockchain solutions provider, EMURGO also provides blockchain education, including courses and expertise for universities, professionals, enterprises, and beginners. EMURGO Academy in India is a prime example of this, attracting students from prominent companies such as Accenture, Bank of America, IBM, Dell, Boeing, GE, Target Corporation, Morgan Stanley, S&P, and many more.

IOHK is an engineering and technology firm that specializes in constructing cryptocurrencies and blockchains for educational institutions, corporations, and governments. The company was established by Charles Hoskinson and Jeremy Wood, and it is responsible for developing, constructing, and sustaining the Cardano platform. IOHK is completely decentralized and consists of creative, dynamic groups located all around the globe. These teams are dedicated to innovation by delivering the highest software engineering standards, based on meticulous peer-reviewed scientific research.

IOHK is an industry leader in the creation of distributed computing systems and decentralized technological solutions. The company is presently exploring new tools and paradigms in the fields of cryptographic research and cryptocurrency architecture. IOHK believes in open-source principles and ethical, purpose-driven business practices. The company creates technology that is beneficial to many, not just a select few. Similar to the Cardano Foundation and EMURGO, IOHK is devoted to promoting blockchain education. IOHK Research is focused on advancing the academic study of blockchain through its team of educators, academic partners, and custom-developed courses.

During the Summit, Cardano announced several major partnerships. One of these was with Veritree, a company specializing in global land restoration and verification of tree planting. Veritree will use Cardano to secure their records and provide transparent and auditable blockchain-based reports on all of their afforestation and reforestation efforts.

Another partnership was formed with Rival, an esports and gaming platform. Together, they plan to develop NFT marketplaces and fan rewards for Rival and its partners. Additionally, Cardano partnered with UBX, a fintech venture studio and fund that launched its own public stake pool on the Cardano network.

Lastly, Cardano formed a partnership with AID:tech, which will utilize the Cardano blockchain to offer identity-based solutions for finance, payments, and insurance.

Cardano also has a number of partnerships and collaborations with leading organizations in various industries, including government, education, and finance. Some examples of partnerships that Cardano has announced include:

In 2021, Cardano announced a partnership with the government of Ethiopia to explore the use of blockchain technology in the country's agriculture sector. In 2020, Cardano announced a partnership with New Balance, a leading sports footwear and apparel company, to explore the use of blockchain technology in the supply chain and manufacturing processes. In 2019, Cardano announced a partnership with the government of Georgia to explore the use of blockchain technology in the country's public services.2018, Cardano announced a partnership with the University of Edinburgh to establish a research center focused on blockchain technology and cryptocurrency. In 2017, Cardano announced a partnership with the Tokyo Institute of Technology to explore the use of blockchain technology in various industries, including finance, healthcare, and supply chain management. These partnerships help to promote the adoption and use of Cardano in a variety of sectors and demonstrate the versatility and potential of the platform.

Chapter 11
Peer Reviewed Research

Cardano (ADA) is a blockchain-based platform that was launched in 2017 by IOHK, a blockchain research and development company. One of the key features of Cardano is its commitment to peer-reviewed research and development, which is aimed at ensuring the platform is secure, scalable, and interoperable.

In the world of blockchain and cryptocurrency, peer-reviewed research is important because it allows for greater transparency and validation of the technology. It involves a process of independent experts scrutinizing the technology and providing feedback on its strengths and weaknesses, as well as potential avenues for improvement.

Cardano's commitment to peer-reviewed research is exemplified by its research and development arm, the IOHK Research team. This team is made up of a group of world-renowned academics and researchers, including several PhDs and professors, who work together to develop and improve the Cardano blockchain platform.

In fact, Cardano is often cited as one of the most academically rigorous blockchain projects, with its research and development process modeled after that of a scientific research project. This includes a system of formal peer review, which involves submitting research papers to experts in the field for evaluation and feedback.

The Cardano platform also uses a proof-of-stake consensus algorithm, which is designed to be more energy-efficient and scalable than traditional proof-of-work algorithms used by other cryptocurrencies. This algorithm was developed based on research conducted by the IOHK Research team, and has been peer-reviewed to ensure its security and reliability.

Overall, Cardano's commitment to peer-reviewed research and development is a key factor in its success and reputation in the blockchain community. By prioritizing transparency and collaboration, Cardano is working towards creating a more secure, scalable, and interoperable blockchain platform that can support a wide range of decentralized applications and use cases.

Cardano's approach to peer-reviewed research and development is unique in the world of blockchain and cryptocurrency. Most blockchain projects prioritize speed and agility over rigorous academic research, leading to potential security vulnerabilities and other issues.

In contrast, Cardano's development process is based on a rigorous research methodology that involves collaboration between academic researchers and blockchain developers. This methodology is called the "Scientific Method," which involves formulating hypotheses, testing them through experimentation, and peer-reviewing the results.

Cardano's research and development arm, the IOHK Research team, includes experts in various fields such as cryptography, distributed systems, game theory, and programming languages. They work together to develop and improve the Cardano blockchain platform, using a formal process of peer-review to ensure the security, scalability, and interoperability of the platform.

The peer-review process involves submitting research papers to independent experts in the field, who review the papers and provide feedback on their validity and usefulness. This feedback is then incorporated into the research, leading to a more collaborative and transparent development process.

Cardano's commitment to peer-reviewed research has also led to several innovations in the blockchain space. For example, the Ouroboros protocol, which is the basis of Cardano's proof-of-stake consensus algorithm, was developed based on research conducted by the IOHK Research team. This protocol has been peer-reviewed and is considered one of the most secure and energy-efficient consensus algorithms in the industry.

Overall, Cardano's focus on peer-reviewed research and development is a key factor in its success and reputation in the blockchain community. By prioritizing scientific rigor and collaboration, Cardano is working towards creating a more secure, scalable, and interoperable blockchain platform that can support a wide range of decentralized applications and use cases.

How they test the Blockchain?

Testing a blockchain is an essential part of its development process, as it helps to ensure that the platform is secure, reliable, and scalable. Here are some of the ways that blockchain developers test their platforms:

Unit testing: This involves testing individual components of the blockchain, such as the consensus algorithm, smart contracts, and transaction processing. Unit testing helps to identify any bugs or errors in the code, and ensures that each component is functioning as intended.

Integration testing: This involves testing how different components of the blockchain interact with each other. For example, developers may test how the consensus algorithm works with the smart contract platform or how the transaction processing system interacts with the blockchain's storage layer.

Functional testing: This involves testing the blockchain's functionality, such as the ability to process transactions, validate blocks, and enforce consensus rules. Functional testing helps to ensure that the blockchain is working as intended and is able to perform the tasks it was designed to do.

Performance testing: This involves testing the blockchain's ability to handle large volumes of transactions and users. Performance testing helps to identify any bottlenecks or scalability issues in the platform, and ensures that the blockchain can handle real-world usage scenarios.

Security testing: This involves testing the blockchain's security features, such as encryption, authentication, and access control. Security testing helps to identify any vulnerabilities or weaknesses in the platform, and ensures that the blockchain is resistant to attacks such as double-spending, 51% attacks, and other potential security threats.

CHAPTER 12
DEX

A DEX, or Decentralized Exchange, is a type of cryptocurrency exchange that operates in a decentralized manner, without the need for intermediaries such as centralized exchanges. In a DEX, users hold their own funds and private keys, allowing for increased security and control over their assets.

In a centralized exchange, users deposit their funds into the exchange's custody, and the exchange holds and manages the user's private keys. This can result in central points of failure and security risks, as centralized exchanges have been subject to hacks and other security threats in the past.

In a DEX, users can trade cryptocurrencies and other decentralized tokens directly with each other, without the need for intermediaries. This provides increased security and privacy, as users are in control of their own funds and private keys. Additionally, DEXs offer increased transparency, as all trades and transactions are recorded on a public blockchain, providing a tamper-proof and transparent record of all activity.

DEXs have become an increasingly popular alternative to centralized exchanges, as they offer increased security and control for users, as well as increased transparency and accessibility. However, DEXs can also have their own unique challenges, such as lower liquidity and slower trade execution times, compared to centralized exchanges. Overall, DEXs represent an important part of the DeFi ecosystem and provide an alternative to traditional centralized exchanges.

Here are a few additional points to keep in mind when it comes to DEXs:

Decentralized Order Books: In a DEX, the order book is maintained by a decentralized network of nodes, rather than by a centralized entity. This allows for increased security and privacy, as users' order information is not held by a centralized party that could be subject to hacks or other security threats.

Trading Pairs: DEXs offer a wide variety of trading pairs, allowing users to trade different cryptocurrencies and decentralized tokens. Some DEXs also offer unique trading pairs that are not available on centralized exchanges, such as token pairs for DeFi platforms or NFTs.

Liquidity Pools: Many DEXs use liquidity pools to provide increased liquidity and more efficient trade execution. In a liquidity pool, users provide their tokens to the pool in exchange for a share of the pool's tokens. This allows the DEX to offer increased liquidity and more efficient trade execution, as trades are executed against the pool's tokens rather than individual users' tokens.

Gas Fees: DEXs operate on the Ethereum network, which requires users to pay gas fees in order to execute trades and interact with the platform. Gas fees can vary depending on network congestion, and users should be aware of the potential costs associated with trading on a DEX.

Market Making: DEXs can offer opportunities for market makers, who provide liquidity to the platform by adding orders to the order book. Market makers can earn rewards for providing liquidity, such as trading fees or token rewards from the DEX.

Overall, DEXs offer an alternative to centralized exchanges, offering increased security, privacy, and transparency for users. While there are unique challenges associated with DEXs, such as lower liquidity and higher gas fees, they represent an important part of the DeFi ecosystem and provide a decentralized alternative for trading cryptocurrencies and decentralized tokens.

Here is a scenario of John using a Decentralized Exchange (DEX):

John has been interested in cryptocurrency for a while and has recently decided to invest some of his savings into the space. He has done some research and has learned about the benefits of using a Decentralized Exchange (DEX) to trade cryptocurrencies.

John sets up a wallet on the DEX and transfers some of his Ethereum (ETH) to the wallet. He then uses the DEX to find the trading pair he wants to trade, in this case, he wants to trade ETH for a new cryptocurrency called XYZ token.

John places a buy order for XYZ tokens at a specific price, which is then added to the DEX's decentralized order book. When another user on the DEX places a sell order for XYZ tokens at the same price, John's order is filled, and the trade is executed.

Since the DEX operates in a decentralized manner, John retains control of his private keys and holds the XYZ tokens in his wallet on the DEX. John can then continue to trade XYZ tokens on the DEX, or he can withdraw the tokens to a different wallet or exchange.

John is impressed with the ease of use and security of the DEX, as he was able to trade cryptocurrencies without the need for intermediaries or centralized parties. He is now more confident in his investments in the cryptocurrency space and is considering using the DEX for future trades.

In this scenario, John has used a DEX to trade cryptocurrencies in a secure and decentralized manner, allowing him to retain control of his assets and trade efficiently and transparently.

liquidity pool is a common feature of decentralized exchanges (DEXs) that provides increased liquidity and more efficient trade execution. In a liquidity pool, users provide their tokens to the pool in exchange for a share of the pool's tokens. These shares are known as liquidity provider (LP) tokens.

The idea behind liquidity pools is to allow users to trade tokens efficiently by pooling their assets together, thereby providing a large pool of liquidity for trades to be executed against. This allows DEXs to offer increased liquidity and more efficient trade execution, as trades are executed against the pool's tokens rather than individual users' tokens.

By providing liquidity to the pool, users earn a share of the trading fees generated by the DEX. Additionally, many DEXs incentivize liquidity providers with additional rewards such as token rewards or interest on their assets.

Overall, liquidity pools play a critical role in the operation of DEXs and help to provide a more seamless trading experience for users. By pooling assets together, liquidity pools provide increased liquidity, lower spreads, and faster trade execution times.

Price Stability: Liquidity pools help to stabilize the price of tokens by providing a large pool of assets for users to trade against. This can reduce the impact of price fluctuations and make it easier for users to trade at the prices they want.

Increased volume: Liquidity pools also help to increase the trading volume on a DEX by providing a large pool of assets for trades to be executed against. This can make it easier for users to trade large quantities of tokens and can help to attract more users to the DEX.

Lower fees: DEXs that use liquidity pools often have lower fees compared to centralized exchanges. This is because the use of liquidity pools allows for more efficient trade execution and reduces the need for intermediaries.

Decentralized governance: Many DEXs with liquidity pools are governed by decentralized autonomous organizations (DAOs), meaning that the rules and policies governing the platform are decided by the users rather than by a centralized party.

Token incentives: Some DEXs incentivize users to provide liquidity to their pools by offering token rewards or interest on the assets in the pool. This can help to attract more users to the platform and increase the pool's overall liquidity.

In conclusion, liquidity pools are an important aspect of the DEX ecosystem and provide a range of benefits for users. By pooling assets together, liquidity pools increase liquidity and make it easier for users to trade efficiently and with reduced spreads. Additionally, users can earn rewards by providing liquidity, such as trading fees or token rewards. It's important for users to understand the risks involved, but overall, liquidity pools are a valuable tool for DEX users.

Chapter 13
DeFi

DeFi, or Decentralized Finance, refers to a new financial ecosystem built on blockchain technology and decentralized networks. It offers alternative financial products and services that are transparent, accessible, and permissionless, providing an alternative to traditional financial systems.

DeFi products and services include decentralized exchanges (DEXs), non-custodial wallets, stablecoins, lending and borrowing platforms, insurance protocols, and many others. These decentralized platforms allow users to interact with each other directly, without the need for intermediaries such as banks or financial institutions.

DeFi aims to offer a more inclusive and open financial system, allowing anyone with an internet connection to participate and access financial services, regardless of their location or credit history. Additionally, DeFi provides increased security and privacy, as users are in control of their own funds and private keys.

Overall, DeFi represents a major shift in the traditional financial system, offering a more decentralized, transparent, and accessible alternative for financial services and products.

How do DEFI work?

DeFi platforms, also known as decentralized finance platforms, work by leveraging blockchain technology and smart contracts to offer financial services that are transparent, accessible, and permissionless. Here's a general overview of how DeFi works:

Decentralized Infrastructure: DeFi platforms are built on decentralized infrastructure, such as blockchain networks, that allow for the creation of trustless financial services and products. This eliminates the need for intermediaries, such as banks, and provides increased security and transparency.

Smart Contracts: DeFi platforms utilize smart contracts, which are self-executing agreements with the terms of the agreement directly written into code. Smart contracts automate the execution of financial transactions and agreements, ensuring that they are executed accurately and securely.

Decentralized Tokens: DeFi platforms use decentralized tokens, such as cryptocurrencies, as a means of value transfer and exchange. Tokens can be used to represent various financial assets, such as stocks, bonds, and commodities, and can be traded and exchanged on decentralized exchanges (DEXs).

Lending and Borrowing: DeFi platforms offer lending and borrowing services, allowing users to lend out their assets to earn interest, or borrow assets for a fee. These services are facilitated by smart contracts and often use decentralized tokens, such as stablecoins, to provide stability and reduce volatility.

Decentralized Exchanges (DEXs): DeFi platforms include decentralized exchanges (DEXs), which allow for the trading of decentralized tokens in a trustless and decentralized manner. DEXs eliminate the need for intermediaries, such as centralized exchanges, and provide increased security and control over funds for users.

Yield Farming: DeFi platforms offer yield farming, a process in which users can earn rewards for providing liquidity to decentralized exchanges (DEXs) or lending platforms. This incentivizes users to provide liquidity to the DeFi ecosystem, helping to increase the overall liquidity and stability of DeFi platforms.

Transparency and Accessibility: DeFi platforms are transparent and accessible, allowing anyone with an internet connection to participate and access financial services, regardless of their location or credit history.

Note that this is a general overview of how DeFi works, and specific DeFi platforms may have slightly different processes and protocols. However, the basic principle remains the same: DeFi platforms leverage decentralized infrastructure, smart contracts, and decentralized tokens to provide an alternative financial ecosystem that is transparent, accessible, and permissionless.

Open-Source Nature: Many DeFi platforms are open-source, meaning that their code is publicly available and can be audited and reviewed by the community. This helps to ensure the security and transparency of DeFi platforms.

High Risk and Volatility: DeFi is still a relatively new and rapidly evolving sector, and as such, it can be associated with high risk and volatility. DeFi platforms and products can be subject to hacks, scams, and other security threats, so it is important for users to thoroughly research and understand the risks involved before investing in DeFi.

Interoperability: DeFi platforms are interoperable, meaning that they can interact with each other and provide a seamless experience for users. For example, a user can borrow from one platform, lend on another platform, and trade on a third platform, all with the same decentralized token.

Regulation: The regulatory landscape for DeFi is still evolving, and it remains to be seen how DeFi platforms and products will be regulated in the future. Currently, some DeFi platforms operate in regulatory grey areas, and it is important for users to be aware of the potential risks associated with these platforms.

Overall, DeFi represents a major shift in the traditional financial system, offering a more decentralized, transparent, and accessible alternative for financial services and products. While there are risks and challenges associated with DeFi, it has the potential to revolutionize finance and provide increased access and opportunities for people around the world.

Chapter 14
DAO

DAO stands for Decentralized Autonomous Organization, which is a decentralized entity run by a set of rules encoded as computer programs on a blockchain network. DAOs are run by the collective decision-making of its members, who use cryptocurrency to vote on proposals and make decisions for the organization. They operate without a central authority, making them transparent and resistant to censorship or control. DAOs have been used for various purposes, such as decentralized exchanges, investment funds, and governance models for decentralized projects.

DAOs operate on the principle of smart contracts, which are self-executing agreements with the terms of the agreement directly written into code. The rules and functioning of the DAO are encoded into the smart contract, and decisions are made through a voting process where members hold and cast votes proportional to the amount of cryptocurrency they hold in the DAO.

DAOs have the potential to disrupt traditional organizational structures by offering a more democratic and transparent model for decision-making and governance. They also offer the potential for lower transaction costs and reduced barriers to entry for participating in the organization.

However, the decentralized nature of DAOs also brings about certain challenges, such as the risk of 51% attacks and the difficulty in changing the rules of the organization once it has been deployed. Despite these challenges, DAOs have gained popularity in the cryptocurrency community as a promising model for decentralized governance.

One of the key benefits of DAOs is their ability to operate in a trustless manner, eliminating the need for intermediaries or centralized authorities. Members of a DAO can participate in the decision-making process directly, without relying on a third party to facilitate transactions or enforce agreements.

Another advantage of DAOs is their ability to raise funds through token offerings. Members can contribute to a DAO by purchasing tokens, which represent ownership and voting rights within the organization. The funds raised can then be used to support the development and growth of the DAO's project or initiative.

However, DAOs also face some challenges and risks. One of the main risks is the possibility of a 51% attack, where a group of members controlling over 51% of the voting power can manipulate the outcome of a vote to their advantage. Additionally, the immutability of the blockchain means that once a DAO is deployed, its rules and structure cannot be easily changed, which can limit its adaptability to changing market conditions.

Despite these challenges, DAOs continue to gain popularity and have been used for various purposes, such as decentralized exchanges, investment funds, and governance models for decentralized projects. As the technology and understanding of DAOs continue to evolve, it is likely that we will see more widespread adoption and innovative use cases in the future.

Here's a step-by-step explanation of how DAOs work:

Creation: A DAO is created by writing a set of rules and protocols into a smart contract on a blockchain network, such as Ethereum. The smart contract serves as the backbone of the DAO, defining how it operates and how decisions are made.

Membership: Members can become part of a DAO by purchasing tokens, which represent ownership and voting rights within the organization. The number of tokens held by a member is proportional to their voting power within the DAO.

Proposals: Members can submit proposals for the DAO to consider. These proposals can be anything from changes to the organization's rules to funding new projects or initiatives.

Voting: Members vote on proposals by casting their tokens in support or opposition. The outcome of the vote is determined by the total number of tokens cast in favor or against the proposal.

Decision-making: If a proposal receives a sufficient number of votes in favor, it is executed automatically by the smart contract. The rules encoded in the smart contract determine the outcome of the proposal, such as the allocation of funds or the implementation of a new rule.

Execution: Once a proposal is passed, it is executed automatically by the smart contract. The rules and protocols encoded in the smart contract determine how the proposal is implemented, such as the transfer of funds or the creation of new tokens.

Transparency: All transactions and decisions made within a DAO are recorded on the blockchain, making them publicly accessible and transparent. This helps to ensure accountability and prevent fraud or manipulation within the organization.

Note that this is a general overview of how DAOs work, and specific DAOs may have slightly different processes and protocols. However, the basic principle remains the same: DAOs are decentralized entities run by smart contracts, allowing for transparent and democratic decision-making by its members.

Chapter 15
About the Founder

Charles Hoskinson, the co-founder of Ethereum and the CEO of Input Output Hong Kong (IOHK), the firm leading the development of Cardano, has made a number of statements about Cardano and its goals. Here are a few quotes from Charles Hoskinson:

"Cardano is a decentralized public blockchain and cryptocurrency project and is fully open source. Cardano is developing a smart contract platform which seeks to deliver more advanced features than any protocol previously developed. It is the first blockchain platform to be built in the Haskell programming language."

"Cardano is a third-generation blockchain platform that aims to deliver a more secure and scalable blockchain platform for the development of decentralized applications (DApps) and smart contracts. Cardano is built on a proof-of-stake (PoS) consensus algorithm and includes a number of advanced features such as formal verification, which allows developers to mathematically prove the correctness of their code."

"Cardano is a project that is built on the values of openness, transparency, and inclusivity. We believe that these values are essential for the development of a global, open financial system that is accessible to all."

"Cardano is a blockchain platform that is designed to be scalable, secure, and flexible, and we believe that it has the potential to become the foundation for a new global financial system that is more open, transparent, and inclusive."

This is what Charles Hoskinson had to say when asked . . .

Why is Cardano going to be so much more successful than a Ethereum?

One of the things about wisdom is… that you tend to develop safety belt after you invent the car and you don't just proactively say..Hi. Still working out the kinks.Hey, it's a good idea to put on the safely belt first and what happens is, you get into a car accident, you go through the windshield…and be like boy.. we should have done something about that.

So, Ethereum and Bitcoin were much smaller systems in a much smaller economy when they came out. So, there was no value and risk. We raised $18 million dollars for Ethereum, we were like wow. If we could get to a hundred million dollar cryptocurrency, you know... few thousand people building cool stuff, successful... hazzaa. Now, it's a hundred and thirty billion dollar ecosystem (a couple of years ago)

So, there is a fundamental difference between where it began to where it's at, and similarly when you build a car, or the first airplane, you're not thinking at all about safety. You're not thinking at all about the successful factors that come, the consequences of success that come. Well, if you build a car today, you don't have the ability to just pretend like history doesn't exist and so you'll have to do things differently.

So, the Teslas for example, had to adhere to all the safety standards of Ford, GM and these other things, while also innovating and bringing new things to market. So, we recognized early on, there were a lot of issues with the consensus design, especially if you plan on scaling with proof-of-work (Ethereum is proof of work) in a way that Bitcoin and Ethereum were using it. So, we needed to do a fundamental different way of using the consensus, and even Vitalik (Ethereum founder) agrees with that, which is why ETH2 exists. They're trying to clean this stuff up. But, we went beyond that and said enitre development paradigm of how people build Dapps, write smart contracts, this type of stuff has to be rethought from the very first principle basis, because it was never built in a way for sustainability. It was never built in a way for resource predictability, because if I am an application builder, I'd like to have predictable application costs. If I was a builder…

Could you imagine web hoast who's like…"Well maybe I'll charge you $500 for your app today and tomorrow it will be $5,000 and the next day it'll be $5."

It's like what kind of drugs are you on? That's not a business. I need to have predictable costs if I'm to have predictable applications or else nothing works. Well, Ethereum was never built for that. It was built as an experiment that kind of grew into a successful project and now, they're trying to build a safer car. And this is why a first mover advantage in technology in many cases is actually at a historic disadvantage (talked about yahoo, Netscape and now Facebook taking a hit from these smaller techs)…So usually what happens with the first *movers, you get a lot of population, but it's unstable and they're very frustrated with that platform.*

And you're covered with lots of scars and legacy design decisions and such things, and as a consequence… it's like holding a sand through your hand, it slips through your fingers. It's really really hard to keep your lead and then all these others competitors come and have the benefit of hindsight and they don't make the same mistakes you've made. They also know where they need to innovate, and they can deal with the legacy concerns you have, they can move faster than you.

As a consequence they get more features on the market before. So for example, Ethereum, have been working on proof-of-stake a year longer than we had with Casper (has to do with scalability and consensus) despite that, we were first to market our proof-of-stake protocol and they probably won't have their turned on until 2022. And that's just completely a consequence of process and scale and dealing with their legacy concerns

References

https://Cardano.org

https://cardanofoundation.org/en/news/hydra-head-protocol-an-open-source-solution-for-scalability/

https://blockworks.co/price/ada

Charles Hoskinson answering question on YouTube

Other online resources

Books by the Author
GT Starr
Available on Amazon and other vendors

Seesaw Derangement Psychological fiction novel about an addict in jail struggling with life after a severe trauma.

Poems of the Addicted Poems written over the years. They relate to addiction, recovery and difficulties. Some are part of the author's creativity.

Twelve Steps In A Nutshell: Workbook Workook designed to help individuals overcome character defects and addictions. It contains multitude of questions and worksheets dealing with recovery and Higher Power as a source of strength that heals and grows

Quest For Answers: Real People with questions- Questions and answers in variety of topic in relation to God, psychogy, behaviors, society and philosophy of life.

www.ingramcontent.com/pod-product-compliance
Lightning Source LLC
LaVergne TN
LVHW051743050326
832903LV00029B/2698